Contents

Bullet train

The front of this train is long and thin. This helps it to go faster.

The train is powered by electricity.

The train has a smooth shape. It can slip through the air easily.

The fastest bullet trains reach speeds of 322 km (200 miles) per hour.

FUN FACTS ● FUN FACTS ● FUN FACTS ● FUN FACTS ● FUN FACTS

It is possible to build faster bullet trains, but they are too noisy to use.

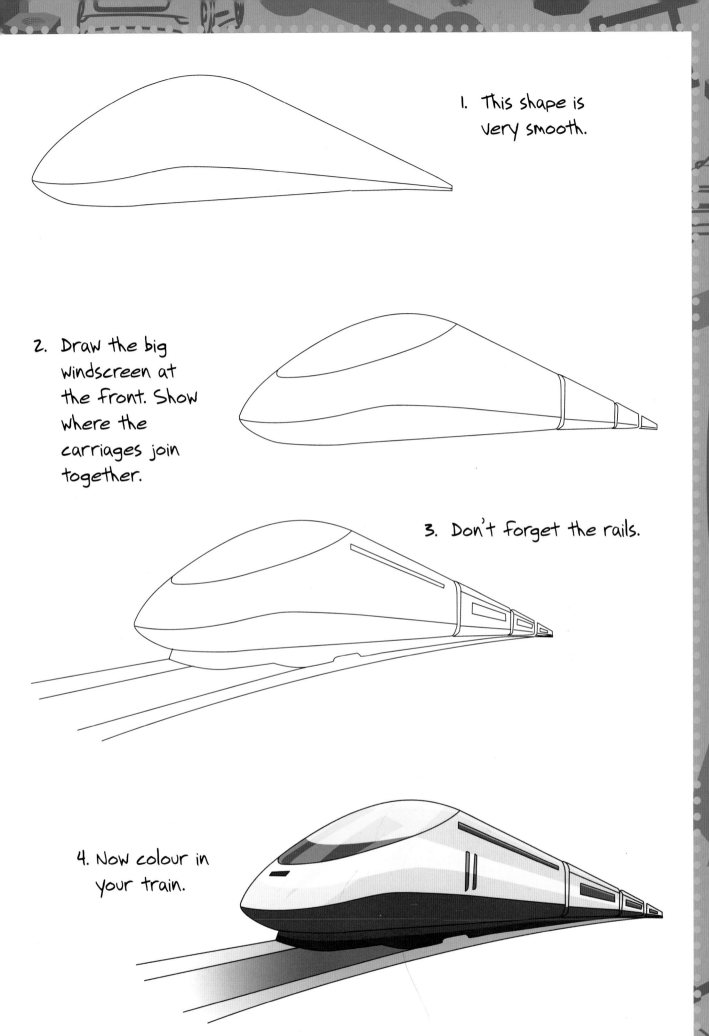

1. This shape is very smooth.

2. Draw the big windscreen at the front. Show where the carriages join together.

3. Don't forget the rails.

4. Now colour in your train.

Racing car

The back wing helps to keep the car on the road.

A racing car has a powerful engine.

This car is very light but strong.

The tyres are very wide. This stops the car from skidding.

FUN FACTS ● FUN FACTS ● FUN FACTS ● FUN FACTS ● FUN FACTS

The controls of the car are all on the steering wheel. The driver can find them quickly and easily.

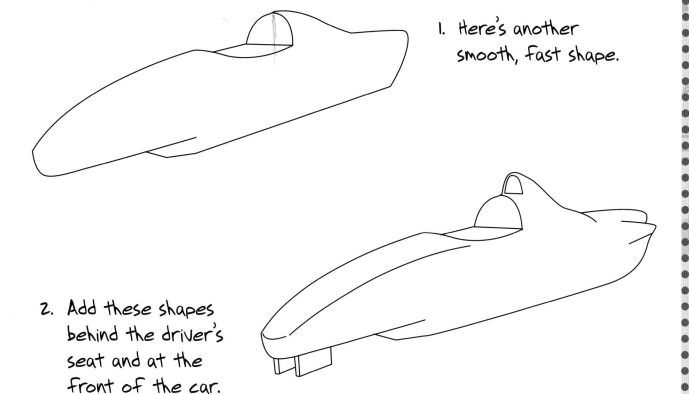

1. Here's another smooth, fast shape.

2. Add these shapes behind the driver's seat and at the front of the car.

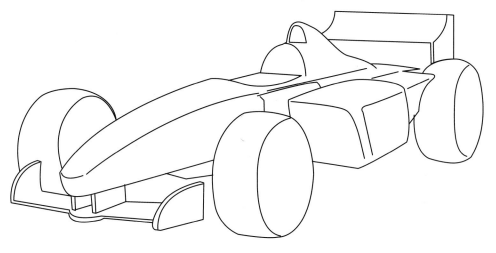

3. Now add some wheels, and the wings at the front and back.

4. Red is a good colour for a racing car.

Speedboat

The windscreen protects the pilot from the air rushing over the boat.

The powerful engine is at the back of the boat.

011

The front of the speedboat lifts up so it isn't touching the water.

FUN FACTS ● FUN FACTS ● FUN FACTS ● FUN FACTS ● FUN FACTS

The world record for the fastest speed on water is 510 km (317 miles) per hour. This record was set in 1978.

1. Draw the top and one side. Make the front pointed so that it can cut through the air easily.

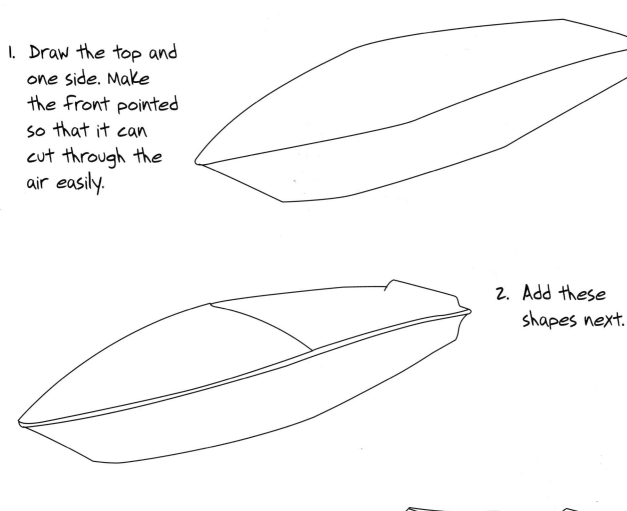

2. Add these shapes next.

3. The windscreen goes at the front.

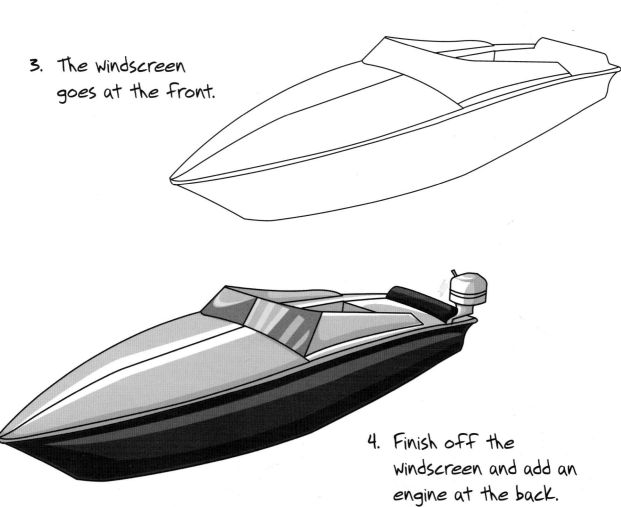

4. Finish off the windscreen and add an engine at the back.

Jet ski

Jet skis are small, fast and easy to drive.

The driver sits here. A passenger can sit behind the driver.

The front of the jet ski pushes water away. The driver should not get too wet.

The engine pushes water out of the back.

FUN FACTS ● FUN FACTS ● FUN FACTS ● FUN FACTS ● FUN FACTS

The driver wears a cord attached to the boat. If he or she falls off, the cord is pulled out and the boat stops.

1. Draw this thin, flat shape for the bottom.

2. The soft seat goes in the middle.

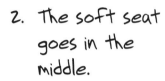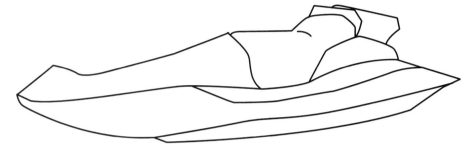

3. Build up the front of the jet ski.

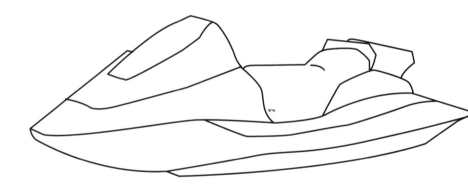

4. Give it handlebars like a motorcycle.

Stealth plane

The plane has four engines. They are inside the wings.

The front is pointed so that it can cut through the air easily.

There is only space for two people inside the plane.

The plane's shape makes it hard for enemies to tell where it is.

FUN FACTS ● FUN FACTS ● FUN FACTS ● FUN FACTS ● FUN FACTS

This plane can fly more than 11,000 km (7,000 miles) before it needs more fuel.

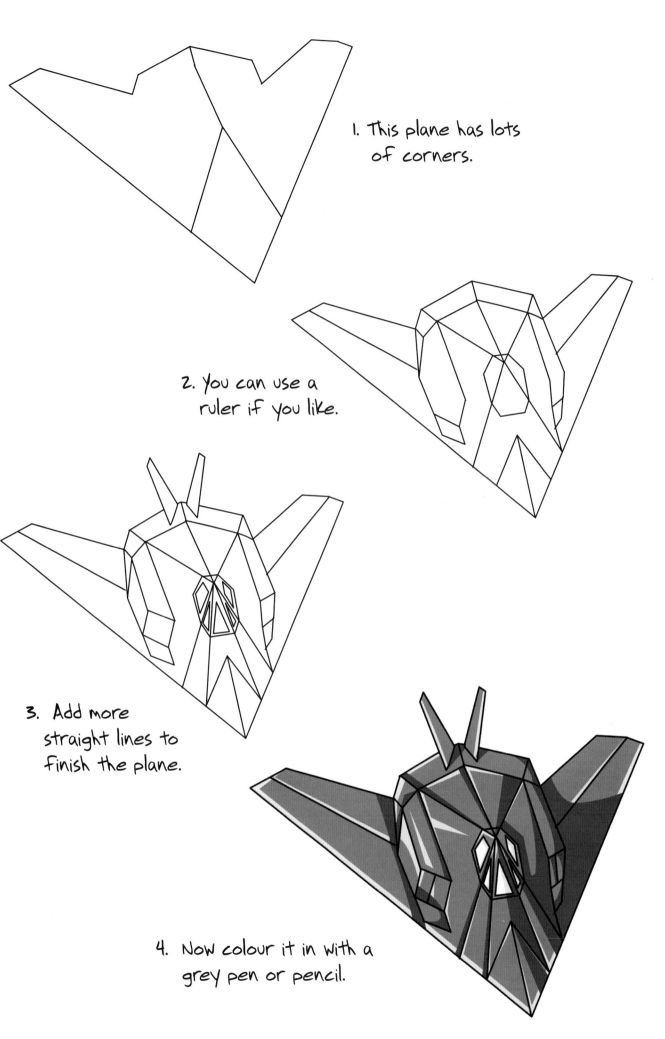

1. This plane has lots of corners.

2. You can use a ruler if you like.

3. Add more straight lines to finish the plane.

4. Now colour it in with a grey pen or pencil.

Quad bike

The driver steers the quad bike with handlebars, like a motorcycle.

Quad bikes can be driven over very bumpy ground.

They can travel at 112 km (70 miles) per hour.

They have four wheels so they don't tip over.

FUN FACTS ● FUN FACTS ● FUN FACTS ● FUN FACTS ● FUN FACTS

Quad bike races take place on roads, over grass, on sand and even on ice!

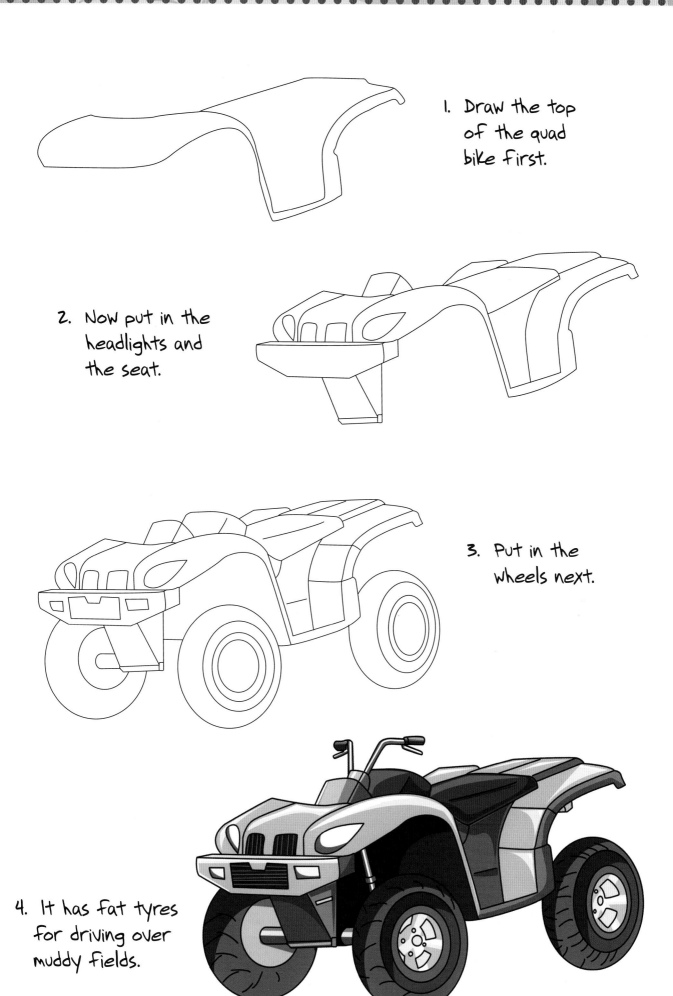

1. Draw the top of the quad bike first.

2. Now put in the headlights and the seat.

3. Put in the wheels next.

4. It has fat tyres for driving over muddy fields.

Fighter plane

This plane can fly at 3,017 km (1,875 miles) per hour.

It can turn very quickly in the air.

The windscreen is also a computer screen.

The pilot can see in all directions.

FUN FACTS ● FUN FACTS ● FUN FACTS ● FUN FACTS ● FUN FACTS

Fighter pilots must be hardworking, healthy and strong.

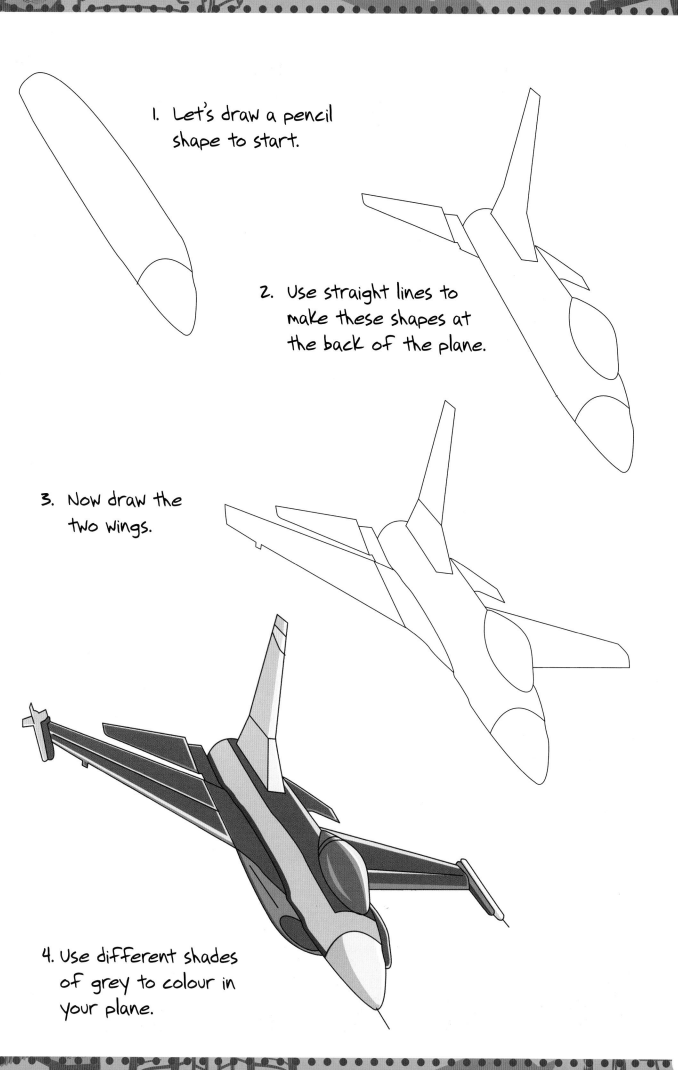

1. Let's draw a pencil shape to start.

2. Use straight lines to make these shapes at the back of the plane.

3. Now draw the two wings.

4. Use different shades of grey to colour in your plane.

Snowmobile

The snowmobile has headlights so that it can be used at night.

The engine turns a track at the back of the snowmobile.

This track can grip the slippery snow.

The skis at the front steer the snowmobile.

FUN FACTS ● FUN FACTS ● FUN FACTS ● FUN FACTS ● FUN FACTS

Some parts of the world are always covered in snow. Snowmobiles are the best way to get around.

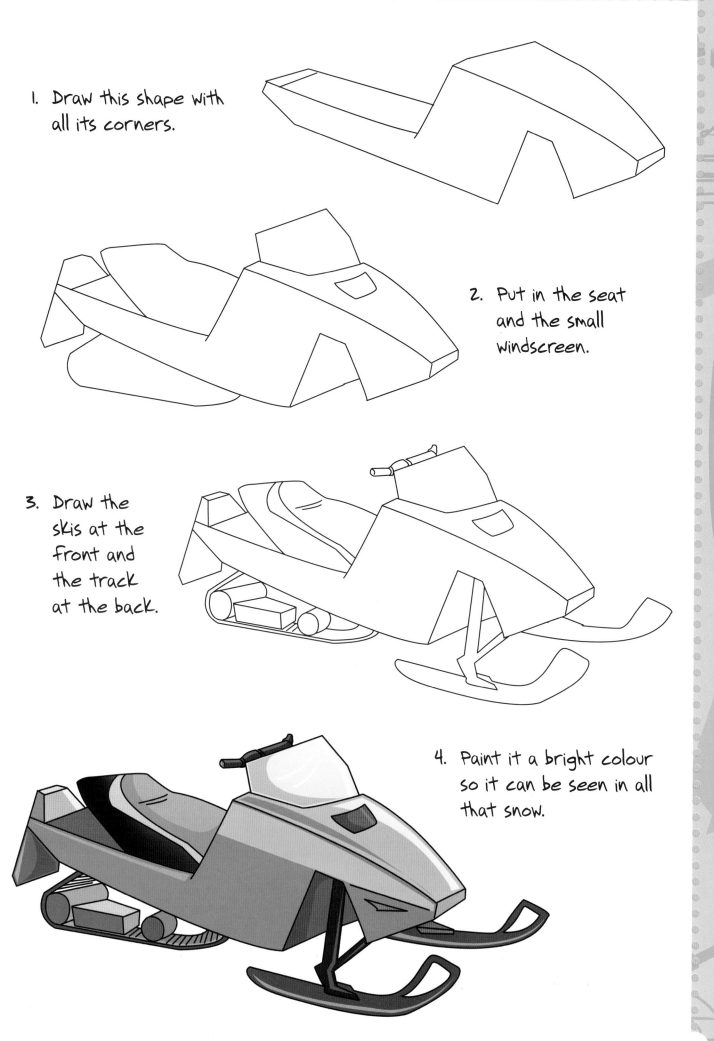

1. Draw this shape with all its corners.

2. Put in the seat and the small windscreen.

3. Draw the skis at the front and the track at the back.

4. Paint it a bright colour so it can be seen in all that snow.

Private jet

Flaps on the plane's wings control its speed and direction.

The engines are at the back of the plane.

This plane only carries about 10 passengers. It is very comfortable inside.

There are lots of windows so the passengers get a good view.

FUN FACTS ● FUN FACTS ● FUN FACTS ● FUN FACTS ● FUN FACTS

This plane can use short runways. This means it can land in places that are impossible for bigger planes.

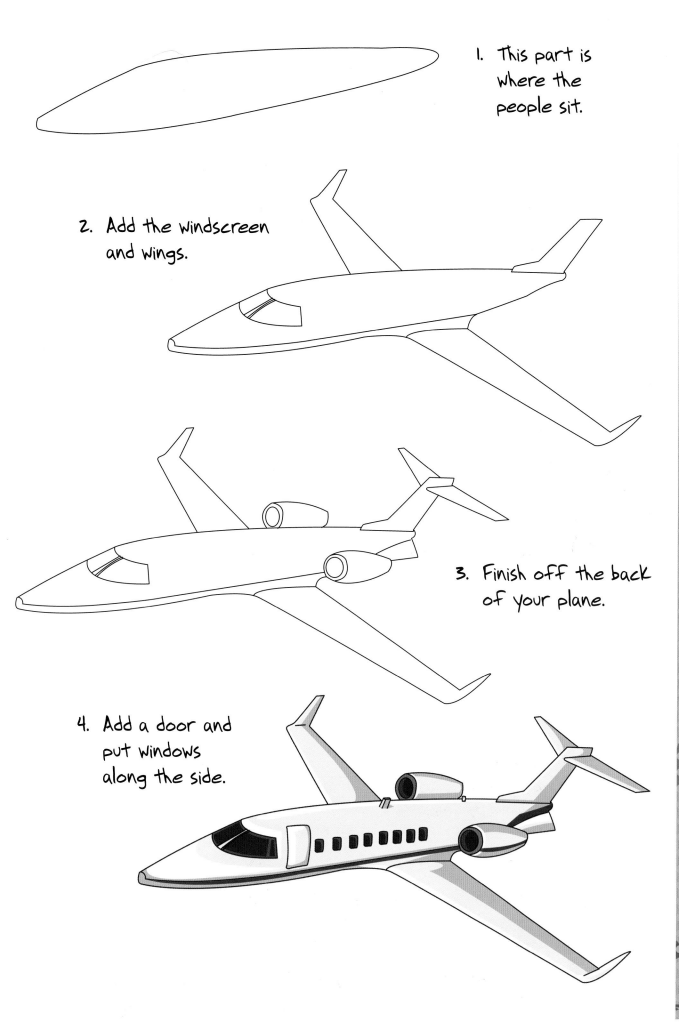

1. This part is where the people sit.

2. Add the windscreen and wings.

3. Finish off the back of your plane.

4. Add a door and put windows along the side.

Kart

The engine is at the back of the kart.

These pedals make the kart go faster or stop.

Bumpers keep the driver from being hurt if a kart crashes.

Karts have small, thick wheels.

FUN FACTS ● FUN FACTS ● FUN FACTS ● FUN FACTS ● FUN FACTS

Many top racing drivers began by racing karts. Drivers as young as eight are able to take part in some kart races.

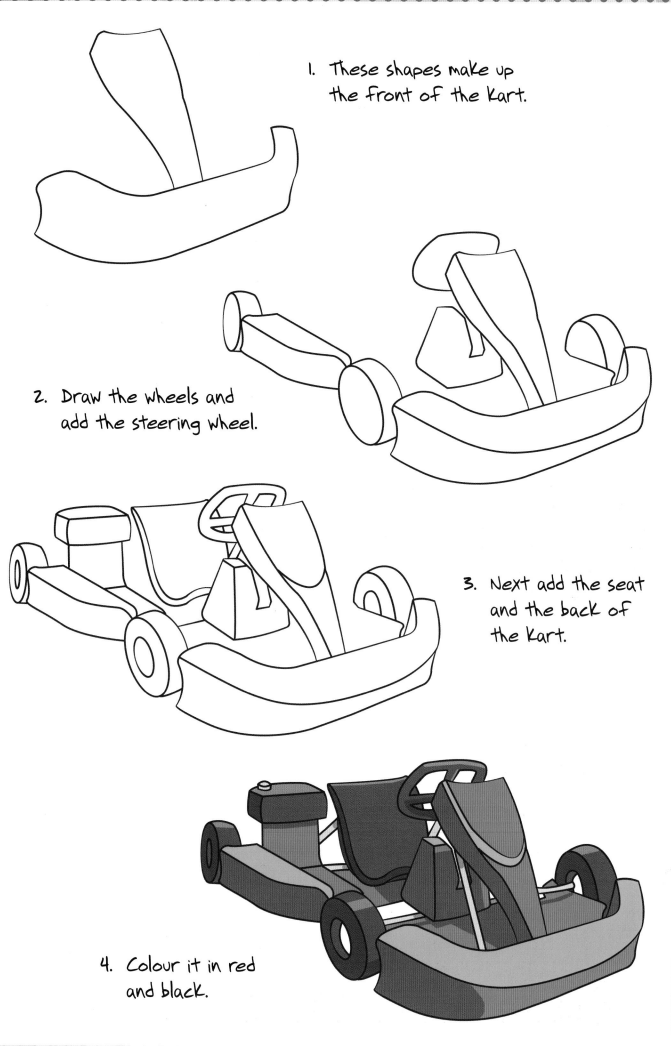

1. These shapes make up the front of the kart.

2. Draw the wheels and add the steering wheel.

3. Next add the seat and the back of the kart.

4. Colour it in red and black.

Scooter

The front of the scooter protects the driver from dust and mud.

There is plenty of space to carry bags.

The small engine is at the back.

The driver's feet rest on this floor.

FUN FACTS ● FUN FACTS ● FUN FACTS ● FUN FACTS ● FUN FACTS

Scooters are great to drive in cities. They can keep moving while cars are stuck in traffic jams.

1. Start with this strange shape.

2. Draw the lines for the seat and handlebars.

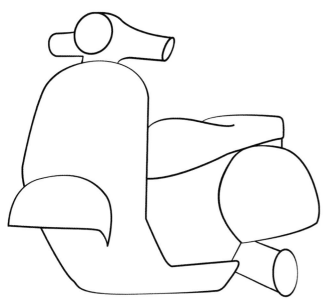

3. Now add the wheels.

4. Before scooting off, add lights and mirrors and colour it in.

Motorcycle and sidecar

A sidecar attaches to the side of a motorcycle, so that a passenger can also go on the trip.

Some sidecars have a roof, but most do not.

A sidecar only has one wheel.

The passenger is very close to the road.

FUN FACTS ● FUN FACTS ● FUN FACTS ● FUN FACTS ● FUN FACTS

Sidecar races are very exciting. The passenger has to climb all over the sidecar and lean out around the bends.

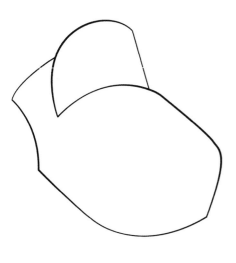

1. Use these shapes to start your motorcycle and sidecar.

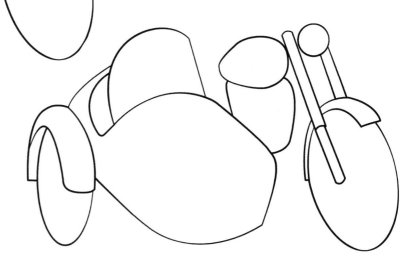

2. Begin to build up the motorcycle, and add a wheel to the sidecar.

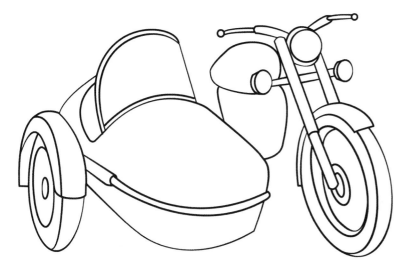

3. Add the lights and handlebars, and draw more circles in the wheels.

4. Fill in the rest of the motorcycle and sidecar, and colour it in.

Stunt plane

A biplane has one wing on top and one wing below.

It has space for two people.

Biplanes have shorter wings than ordinary planes.

The propeller moves the plane forward through the air.

FUN FACTS ● FUN FACTS ● FUN FACTS ● FUN FACTS ● FUN FACTS

Planes with propellers are good at flying at slow speeds. People can easily see as the plane twists and turns in the air.

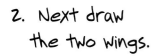

1. Start with a curved shape for the body.

2. Next draw the two wings.

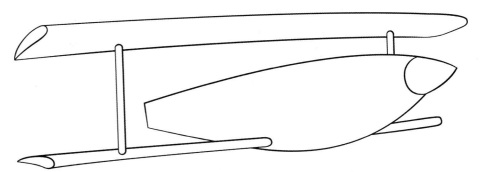

3. Now it's starting to look more like a plane.

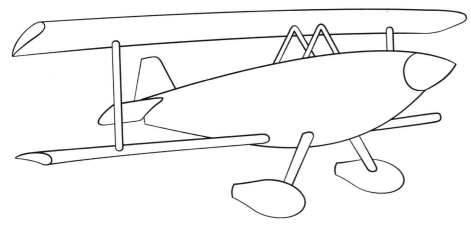

4. Add a propeller and choose bright colours to make the plane fly off the page.

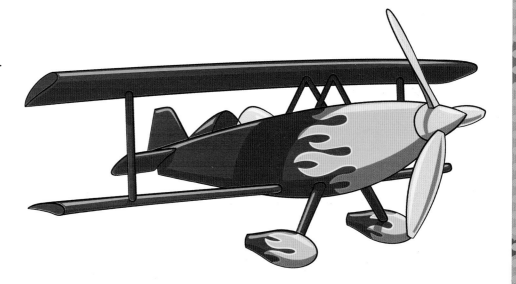

Sports car

The roof folds away with the press of a button.

This bar can carry the weight of the car if it rolls over in a crash.

There is only space for two people in this car.

These holes take air to the engine to help it work.

FUN FACTS ● FUN FACTS ● FUN FACTS ● FUN FACTS ● FUN FACTS

This car has a top speed of almost 322 km (200 miles) per hour.

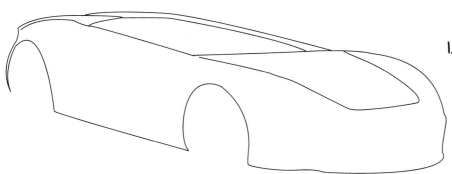

1. This car shape is very curved.

2. See how the wheels tuck into the body.

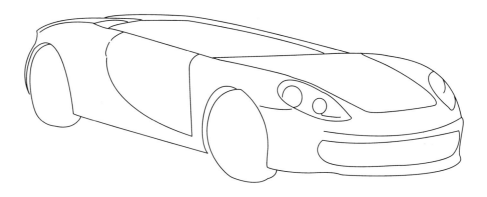

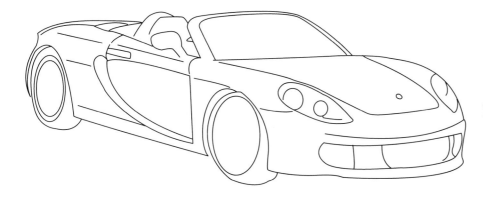

3. Add the windscreen and the passenger seat.

4. Now your car is ready to colour in.

Glossary

bumper something that protects a vehicle in a crash

engine a machine that makes a car, boat or plane move

handlebars the part of a vehicle, such as a motorcycle, that you hold to steer

passenger a person who is in a vehicle, but who is not driving

pedal the part of a machine that is controlled by pushing with your feet

pilot the driver of a plane or a boat

propeller blades that are turned around by an engine to move a plane or boat forward

runway a smooth, level path where aircraft take off and land

track a belt that moves a vehicle over the ground

vehicle a car, boat, plane or other machine used to move people around

windscreen the glass screen protecting the driver

Further Reading

Cars, Trucks, Trains & Planes You Can Draw by Linda Ragsdale (Lark Books, 2008)

Junior How to Draw Cars, Trucks and Planes by Kate Thomson and Barry Green (Top That! Publishing plc, 2011)

You Can Draw Planes, Trains, and Other Vehicles by Brenda Sexton (Picture Window Books, 2011)

Websites

How to draw cars:
http://tlc.howstuffworks.com/family/how-to-draw-cars.htm

How to draw a plane:
http://www.drawingnow.com/learn-to-draw-an-airplane.html

How to draw motorcycles:
http://www.my-how-to-draw.com/how-to-draw-motorcycles.html

Index